EMPIRES IN THE MIDDLE AGES

THE ISLAMIC CALIPHATE

EDITED BY
CAROLYN DeCARLO

Britannica®
Educational Publishing

IN ASSOCIATION WITH

Published in 2018 by Britannica Educational Publishing (a trademark of Encyclopædia Britannica, Inc.) in association with The Rosen Publishing Group, Inc. 29 East 21st Street, New York, NY 10010

Distributed exclusively by Rosen Publishing.
To see additional Britannica Educational Publishing titles, go to rosenpublishing.com.

First Edition

Britannica Educational Publishing
J.E. Luebering: Executive Director, Core Editorial
Andrea R. Field: Managing Editor, Compton's by Britannica

Rosen Publishing
Carolyn DeCarlo: Editor
Nelson Sá: Art Director
Brian Garvey: Designer
Cindy Reiman: Photography Manager
Nicole DiMella: Photo Researcher

Library of Congress Cataloging-in-Publication Data

Names: DeCarlo, Carolyn, editor.
Title: The Islamic Caliphate / edited by Carolyn DeCarlo.
Description: New York : Britannica Educational Publishing, in Association with Rosen Educational Services, 2018. | Series: Empires in the Middle Ages | Includes bibliographical references and index. | Audience: Grades 5-8.
Identifiers: LCCN 2017019759 | ISBN 9781680487831 (library bound : alk. paper) | ISBN 9781680488647 (pbk. : alk. paper) | ISBN 9781680488654 (6 pack : alk. paper)
Subjects: LCSH: Islamic Empire--History--Juvenile literature. | Umayyad dynasty—Juvenile literature. | Abbasids—Juvenile literature. | Fatimites—Juvenile literature.
Classification: LCC DS38.3 .I833 2018 | DDC 909/.09767—dc23
LC record available at https://lccn.loc.gov/2017019759

Manufactured in China

CONTENTS

For several hundred years, the Muslim community and its land formed a state called the Caliphate. The Caliphate was created in 632 CE to prevent a leadership crisis brought on by the death of Muhammad, the founder of Islam. The successor chosen was Abu Bakr, Muhammad's father-in-law and closest adviser. His title was "caliph," a term that means both "successor" and "deputy." The Caliphate lasted until 1258, when the Mongol conquest of Baghdad effectively ended the empire.

The followers of Islam believed they had a mission to spread their religion. They conquered surrounding territories in order to do so. In addition to being religious leaders, therefore, the caliphs were also political rulers of an increasingly large empire. During its first two centuries, the empire grew rapidly to include not only Arabia (the birthplace of Islam) but also most of Southwest Asia, North Africa, and Spain. The Caliphate expanded through military conquests and treaties. Resistance to the Caliphate tended to be only slight and nondestructive, and some areas surrendered without fighting.

The Caliphate began with and was ruled by Arab Muslims. As the empire

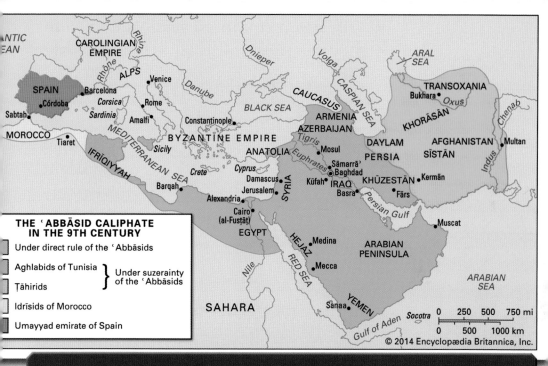

This map depicts the territories held by the Abbasid Caliphate in the ninth century, at the height of the empire.

grew, people of many different cultures and religions were absorbed under its rule. In fact, Arabs came to be in the minority. Many people in the conquered territories kept their own religion, but large numbers converted to Islam. Jews, Christians, and people of other tolerated religions were generally allowed to practice their faith, but they had to pay a special tax. People of other religions were forced to convert to Islam.

As the Caliphate became increasingly prosperous, Islam, Islamic culture, and the Arabic language became prestigious. The more the Muslim rulers were

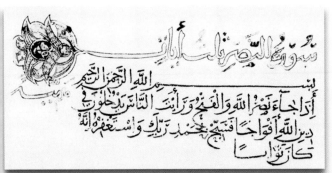

This example of *naskhi* script, a calligraphic style developed in the tenth century for writing in Arabic, is printed in a copy of the Quran found in Baghdad, c. 1000.

successful, the more the people within the empire wanted to adopt the customs of the ruling class. Many people converted to Islam because membership in the Muslim community offered the best chance for social advancement. Arabic was used as the language of Islam and the government, as well as of literature, scholarship, and other high culture. Arabic was also widely adopted as a *lingua franca*—a second, common language—that allowed different peoples throughout the empire to communicate with one another.

During the first 250 years of the Caliphate, Islam was thus transformed from the religion of a small Arab ruling class to the dominant faith of a vast empire. As a result of this long, gradual period of conversion, Arab cultures intermingled with the cultures of the conquered peoples to produce a new Muslim civilization. The Arabs came to rule over a rich complex of old cultures; they introduced new cultural elements, and reoriented old ones in creative ways.

Pilgrims visit the Prophet's Mosque in the holy city of Medina, Saudi Arabia. The mosque holds the tomb of Muhammad.

Over its history, the Caliphate was ruled by many caliphs. Abu Bakr, the first caliph, was from Muhammad's tribe, the Quraysh. Later generations believed the head of the Islamic community had to be from the Quraysh tribe. The continuity of descent within the tribe did not, however, mean that the caliphate (the office of caliph) passed in unbroken succession over the centuries; there were several succeeding—and sometimes simultaneous—caliphates representing different clans within the tribe. For historical clarity, four distinct caliphates may be noted: the Rightly Guided, the Umayyad, the Abbasid, and the Fatimid. In addition, a number of local dynasties opposed the caliphs or simply ignored them.

THE RIGHTLY GUIDED CALIPHATE

The first four caliphs were Abu Bakr, Umar I, Uthman (a member of the Umayyad clan), and Ali, cousin and son-in-law of Muhammad. Collectively, the four are known in Arabic as *al-khulafa' al-rashidun*, or the "rightly guided caliphs." These caliphs were the formative leaders of the Muslim community, or *ummah*.

ABU BAKR, FIRST CALIPH

Abu Bakr (573–634) was the father-in-law and closest companion of the Prophet Muhammad, the founder of Islam. Like Muhammad, Abu Bakr was born in the Arabian town of Mecca, now in Saudi Arabia. His daughter Aishah became one of Muhammad's wives. He was chosen as Muhammad's companion on his journey to Medina, known as the *hijrah*, in 622 CE. In Medina, he served as Muhammad's chief advisor.

Muhammad's father-in-law, Abu Bakr, is depicted mourning the death of the Prophet in this sixteenth-century copy of a manuscript from 1368.

Upon Muhammad's death in 632, the Muslims of Medina resolved the crisis of succession by accepting Abu Bakr as the first caliph. Abu Bakr assumed the Prophet's political and administrative functions. He thereby initiated the Caliphate and began the spread of Islam as a world religion. During his rather brief rule, from 632 to 634, he suppressed the tribal political and religious uprisings known as the *riddah*. He thus brought central Arabia under Muslim control. He then expanded his rule into Iraq and Syria, beginning a series of conquests that spread Islam far beyond Arabia.

Several precedents were set in the selection of Abu Bakr, including that of choosing a member of the Quraysh tribe as caliph. In fact, the first four caliphs, whose reigns constituted what later generations of Muslims would often remember as a golden age of pure Islam, largely established the administrative and judicial organization of the Muslim community and forwarded the policy begun by Muhammad of expanding the Islamic religion into new territories. During the 630s, Syria, Jordan, Palestine, and Iraq were conquered; Egypt was taken from Byzantine control in 645; and frequent raids were launched into North Africa, Armenia, and Persia.

UMAR THE CONQUEROR

Before his death, Abu Bakr nominated Umar ibn Al-Khattab to succeed him. Along with Abu Bakr,

AISHAH: DAUGHTER, WIFE, WARRIOR

Aishah Bint Abi Bakr (614–678) was the third and most favored wife of the Prophet Muhammad. While all Muhammad's marriages had political motivations—in this case, the intention was to cement ties with her father, Abu Bakr, one of Muhammad's most important supporters—it was said that the genuine nature of their relationship was not lessened by his subsequent marriages. Muhammad remained steadfast to Aishah, despite claims from his enemies that she was unfaithful.

When Muhammad died, Aishah became a childless widow at eighteen. While she had wielded no major political power during Muhammad's lifetime, she went on to play a role of some consequence after the Prophet's death. During Uthman's reign from 644 to 656, she was key in fueling the opposition that led to

Here Aishah can be seen riding into the Battle of the Camel, in this manuscript c. 1425.

his murder. She led an army against his successor, Ali, but was defeated in the Battle of the Camel—an engagement that derived its name from the fierce fighting centered around Aishah's mount. Captured, she was allowed to live quietly in Medina, where she died in 678.

Umar was one of the Prophet's chief advisers. Umar I became the second Muslim caliph, under whom Arab armies conquered Mesopotamia and Syria and began the conquest of Iran and Egypt. As caliph, he was the first to call himself "commander of the faithful." His reign saw the transformation of the Islamic state from an Arabian principality to a world power.

Throughout this remarkable expansion, Umar closely controlled general policy and laid down the principles for administering the conquered lands. The structure of the later Islamic empire, including legal practice, is largely due to him. Assassinated by a Persian slave for personal reasons, he died in Medina ten years after coming to the throne. A strong ruler, stern toward offenders, and himself ascetic to the point of harshness, he was universally respected for his justice and authority.

UTHMAN

Uthman ibn Affan, third caliph to rule after the death of the Prophet, was born into the powerful and rich Umayyad clan, considered Meccan aristocracy.

Uthman became the first convert to Islam of high social and economic standing. Muhammad valued this contact, and Uthman married one of his daughters. By Umar's death in 644, Uthman was elected successor—a compromise between more powerful candidates than himself, who canceled each other out.

As caliph, Uthman centralized the administration of the Caliphate and established an official version of the Quran. He continued the conquests that had

A page from one of the oldest surviving copies of the Quran, dating to the Abbasid Caliphate, late eighth century. Early Islamic manuscripts of the Quran are distinguished by their parchment pages, angular scripts, and horizontal formats.

steadily increased the size of the Islamic empire, and he tried to create a central authority rather than the loose tribal alliance that had emerged under Muhammad. To achieve this, he established a system of landed fiefs, distributing many provincial governorships to members of his own family. Thus, much of the treasure received by the central government went to Uthman's family and to other provincial governors rather than to the army.

Uthman was opposed by the army, and by 650, rebellions had broken out in the provinces of Egypt and Iraq. He was killed by rebels in 656. Uthman is critically important in Islamic history because his death marked the beginning of open religious and political conflicts within the Islamic community.

ALI, A CONTROVERSIAL LEADER

Ali ibn Abi Talib was elected caliph after his predecessor, Uthman, was murdered. Members of Uthman's Umayyad clan called for revenge against his murderers, but Ali failed to satisfy their requests. As a result, one member of the Umayyad clan, Muawiyah I, began a rebellion against Ali.

Others who rebelled against Ali were former supporters who became known as Kharijites, or Seceders. They denied the inherent right of the Quraysh tribe to hold the caliphate. They believed that the office should be the reward of "piety," or "dutifulness in

religion," not birth. Ali's followers, however, believed that the caliphs, in addition to being members of the Quraysh, must also be direct descendants of Muhammad through the marriage of Ali and his wife Fatimah, Muhammad's daughter. It was a member of the Kharijites who killed Ali in 661.

A TIME OF STRIFE

The thirty-year period of the rightly guided caliphs, from 632 to 661, was a time of strife that had two momentous consequences for Islam. First, Ali moved

The Blue Mosque is a well-known site in Mazar-e Sharif, Afghanistan. According to an Afghan legend, it marks the burial place of Ali, son-in-law of the Prophet Muhammad.

his capital to Iraq. The capital never returned to Arabia; thus, the whole administrative organization for running the empire, as well as most of the cultural flowering of Islam, was no longer in the religion's heartland. Arabia gradually became a remote province within the scope of the empire.

Second, and especially significant for the history of Islam, was the murder of Ali. This resulted in a major split in Islam, as the party—*shi'at* in Arabic—of Ali came to constitute a separate branch with distinctive beliefs and practices. The split between the Shiites and the group that became known as the Sunni originated

17

EARLY ISLAMIC LITERATURE

The religious zeal of the early Muslims inspired the beginning of two significant works, collections that were not completed until later centuries. The most important was the *hadith*, the record of the sayings and deeds of Muhammad. The sudden death of the spiritual and political leader took the Islamic community by surprise, and within a few decades it was deemed necessary to preserve all of Muhammad's words and actions since they were believed to have been inspired. By the ninth century, the hadith had been solidified into a body of material to which no new traditions were added. In the modern era, the hadith is still revered as a major source of religious law and moral guidance, second only to the Quran.

Another collection that was begun at the same time consists of the sayings of Ali, Muhammad's son-in-law and the fourth caliph, whose followers later established a major division in Islam, Shia. Finally compiled in the tenth century, the collection is called *The Road of Eloquence*. It is a masterpiece of Arabic prose that has inspired numerous commentaries and imitations in other languages.

as a dispute over the authority of Ali to rule as caliph. By 661, Ali's rival, Muawiyah I, a fellow member of Uthman's Umayyad clan, had wrested away the Caliphate, and his rule established the Umayyad Caliphate that lasted until 750.

CHAPTER 2

THE UMAYYAD CALIPHATE

By the time of Ali's death, his prestige had severely declined, while Muawiyah had built up a strong military force. In 661, Muawiyah became the first caliph of the Umayyad line. Muawiyah selected his son, Yazid I (reign 680–683), to succeed him.

It was not always smooth sailing for the Umayyads, though; three caliphs ruled in quick succession between 680 and 685. In fact, the nearly one hundred years of Umayyad rule were further divided between two

A detail of a mosaic from the Umayyad Mosque, also known as the Great Mosque of Damascus, located in Syria. After the conquest of Damascus in 634, the mosque was built on the site of a Christian basilica.

POETRY AS POLITICAL

The rise of sectarian rivalries in the Caliphate contributed to an emerging trend in poetry, which became a favorite mode of expression for differing points of view. The three greatest poets of the Umayyad period were all polemicists who used their verses to support political factions.

Jarir and al-Farazdaq (Tammam ibn Ghalib Abu Firas) were active at the courts of the Umayyad caliphs and ardent supporters of the regime. The two were enemies, however, and they delighted rival tribesmen with their stinging satires against each other. The work of these two poets has furnished historians with a rich vein of material on the social and political climate of Islam during the early eighth century. They used the traditional *qasida* form with great effect, incorporating a wealth of vocabulary and imagination. The poetry of the third great poet of the Umayyad period, al-Akhtal, is also highly political. Though he was a Christian, al-Akhtal was a strenuous supporter of the policies of the first Umayyad, Muawiyah I, and his verses often skewered those who opposed them.

branches of the family—the Sufyanid, which reigned from 661 to 684, and the Marwanid, which reigned from 684 to 750, the end of the Umayyad Caliphate.

UMAYYAD STRENGTHS

Abd al-Malik became the fifth caliph (685–705) of the Umayyad Arab dynasty. He succeeded in reestablishing the authority of the Umayyad capital of Damascus (in Syria) after nearly twenty years of military campaigning. The Syrian army became the Umayyads' military support, enabling them to expand the empire while simultaneously controlling Arab factions. Abd al-Malik reorganized and strengthened governmental administration and, throughout the empire, adopted Arabic as the language of administration. He is also remembered for building the Dome of the Rock in Jerusalem; the shrine is located at the site where the Prophet Muhammad is traditionally believed to have ascended into heaven.

The Dome of the Rock is a Muslim shrine in the Old City of Jerusalem.

Under his son al-Walid (705–715), Muslim forces took permanent possession of North Africa, converted the native Berbers to Islam, and overran most of the Iberian Peninsula as the Visigothic kingdom there collapsed. Progress was also made in the east with settlement in the Indus River valley. Al-Walid is best known for the mosques constructed during his reign. Fervently orthodox in his religious views, he had a great interest in architecture. As caliph, he confiscated the Christian Basilica of St. John the Baptist in Damascus and had the Great Mosque (Umayyad Mosque)

The Great Mosque of Damascus, or Umayyad Mosque, stands in the Old City of Damascus, Syria.

erected on the site. He also had mosques built at Medina and Jerusalem.

TRIBAL RIVALRIES

The decline of Umayyad power began in 717, when its armies suffered a serious defeat at the hands of the Byzantine emperor, Leo III. The dynasty was further weakened by financial troubles—the vast expenditures of the caliphs were not being readily replaced through taxation. Another difficulty was the matter of ruling so large an empire from a capital so far removed from the frontiers. Local centers of power appeared, spurred by tribal rivalries and general hostility to the Caliphate from the various sects.

Umayyad power had never been firmly seated, and the Caliphate disintegrated rapidly after the long reign of al-Malik (724–743). Most of the agitation against the last Umayyads was coordinated by a clan descended from an uncle of Muhammad, al-Abbas. Through a well-organized network of secret agents, this clan succeeded in capitalizing on resentment against the Umayyads. Between 745 and 747 revolts broke out in Syria, Iraq, and Khorasan (centered in what is now northeastern Iran). By 749, the rebels were strong enough to proclaim their leader, Abu al-Abbas al-Saffah, as caliph.

The last Umayyad, Marwan II, was defeated in the Battle of Great Zab (750) by the followers of the

The Mosque-Cathedral in Córdoba, Spain. Also known as the Mezquita, the great Mosque-Cathedral hints at an age when Muslims, Jews, and Christians lived side by side, influencing each other's designs and cultures.

Abbasid family; he fled to Egypt, where he was killed. The remaining members of the Umayyad clan were hunted down and murdered. One, however, escaped: Abd al-Rahman made his way to Spain and—with the help of Umayyad supporters—established the Umayyad dynasty of Córdoba. This dynasty declared itself a caliphate in 929 and ruled Spain until 1031. Spain was subsequently ruled by other Muslim dynasties until 1492.

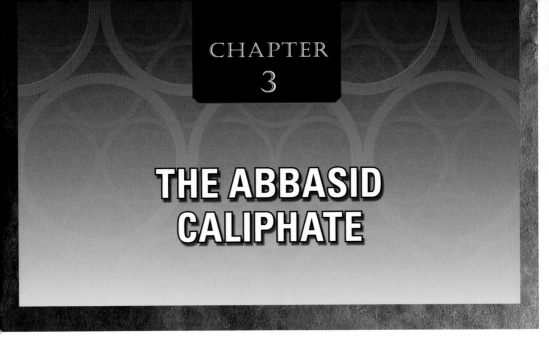

THE ABBASID CALIPHATE

The installation of the Abbasids in 750 significantly changed the nature of the Caliphate. The Abbasid dynasty ruled from 750 to 1258, a period during which Arab-Muslim culture and scholarship merged with Persian administration and arts. Because the base of support for the revolt against the Umayyads had come from eastern provinces, the capital was moved from Damascus to Baghdad, Iraq, a center of communications with both the rest of Iraq and Persia (Iran). The Abbasid Caliphate turned eastward, to Iraq, Persia, India, and Central Asia. This perhaps unintentional neglect of the Mediterranean provinces led to a weakening of the Caliphate's power there.

A CAPITAL IN BAGHDAD

The first Abbasid caliph, al-Saffah, died in 754 and was succeeded by his brother, al-Mansur (reign 754–775).

An image of modern-day Baghdad, Iraq. The capital of the Islamic empire was moved from Damascus to Baghdad during the Abbasid Caliphate. This change strengthened communications with the rest of Iraq and Persia.

Al-Mansur managed to put down revolts against the Caliphate and to get rid of his enemies. It was he who transferred the capital to Baghdad, which remained the leading commercial, cultural, and social city of Islam until the Fatimids raised Cairo, Egypt, to a similar status in the tenth century.

The next Abbasid, al-Mahdi (reign 775–785), attempted to win over the Shiite Muslims but was unsuccessful. Revolts continued against the dynasty for many years. After the brief reign of al-Mahdi's son al-Hadik (785–786), an individual was installed who began what has been called the Golden Age of Islam: Harun al-Rashid.

THE GOLDEN AGE OF ISLAM

Harun ruled from 786 to 809, and it is his reign that was so richly romanticized in the *Arabian Nights*, one of the masterpieces of Islamic literature. Much of the wealth of the Caliphate poured into

This sixteenth-century Persian School miniature depicts Caliph Harun al-Rashid at the baths.

his court. Nevertheless, during his rule, the kingdom seethed with unrest and rebellion. To assure stability in one part of the empire, Harun granted the governor of an African province (now Tunisia) the right to rule in return for an annual tribute. The governor subsequently won the right to nominate his son as his successor, and in so doing he managed to set up a separate line of rulers that lasted for more than a century. This action set a precedent for the falling away in distant provinces from allegiance to the Caliphate,

THE STORIES OF SCHEHERAZADE

The colorful tales called the *Arabian Nights*, also known as *The Thousand and One Nights*, give an idea of life in the court of one of the most famous Abbasid caliphs, Harun al-Rashid. Nobody is sure who first told the tales or where. The stories include those about Sinbad the Sailor, Ali Baba and the forty thieves, and Aladdin and his magic lamp.

The legendary heroine of the tales of the *Arabian Nights* is a girl named Scheherazade, a daughter of the grand vizier (chief minister) of a kingdom somewhere between Arabia and China. The ruler of her kingdom is a cruel sultan who decrees that he will take a new wife each night and have her executed the next morning. Scheherazade conceives a plan to put an end to the daily executions. She marries the sultan, and each evening she tells a story, stopping just when she reaches the most interesting point. To hear the end of the tale, the sultan must let Scheherazade live for another night. Scheherazade keeps telling him stories in this manner for a thousand and

Aladdin, a character in the *Arabian Nights*, holds his magic lamp. This picture is from a 1912 version of the story "Aladdin and the Magic Lamp."

one nights. In the end, the sultan realizes Scheherazade's wisdom, and he revokes his barbaric decree.

During the latter part of the eighth century, the stories of the *Arabian Nights* were introduced into the court of Harun al-Rashid. The storytellers of his court flattered the caliph by making him the hero of many of the tales. Harun liked to disguise himself and roam among his subjects in the streets of Baghdad. It is in this role that he usually appears in the *Arabian Nights*, which also includes descriptions of the fabulous wealth of Harun's court.

a process that began to speed up by the end of the ninth century.

If the reputation of Harun has become overblown because of the *Arabian Nights*, that of his son al-Mamun (reign 813–833) has not been sufficiently praised. The real golden age of the Caliphate came during al-Mamun's reign. He put down rebellions in Egypt, Syria, Armenia, and Khorasan and waged war against the Byzantine Empire. He also made a determined attempt to make peace with the Shiites, but to no avail.

Al-Mamun's interest in the arts and sciences led him to build observatories for the study of astronomy. He also opened a House of Wisdom in Baghdad devoted to the translation of ancient scientific and philosophical works from Greek and other languages. This undertaking provided a channel through which older thought could enter Islamic societies. Muslim scholars in Eurasia and Africa then built on this learning

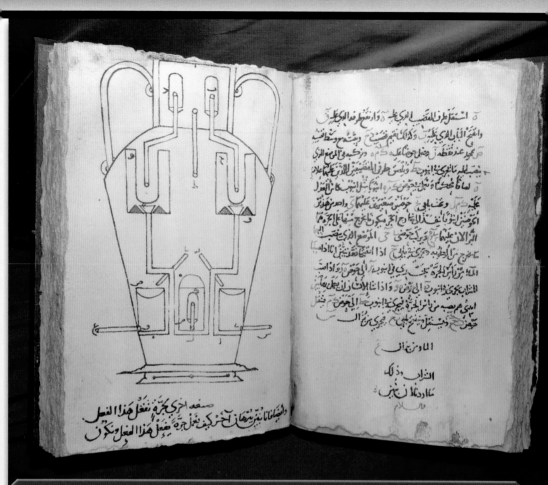

The Book of Ingenious Devices is a large illustrated work on mechanical devices, including automata, published in 850 by three Iranian brothers working at the House of Wisdom in Baghdad, under the Abbasid Caliphate. The Banu Musa brothers, Muhammad, Ahmad, and al-Hasan, are regarded as founders of the Arabic school of mathematics.

and made important new contributions to philosophy, medicine, science, and mathematics.

The Muslim astronomer and mathematician al-Khwarizmi, for example, creatively combined Indian and Greek concepts. He introduced Hindu-Arabic numerals (1, 2, 3, 4, 5, 6, 7, 8, 9, and 0) and the concepts of algebra into European mathematics. Arabic translations of ancient scholarship greatly contributed to the later revival of learning in Europe. Ancient Greek texts were eventually translated from Arabic into Latin, and classical learning made its way into European countries such as Spain, France, and Italy. The Abbasids were also generous patrons of artists and artisans of all kinds. Literature flourished under their rule. Muslim travelers explored Eurasia and Africa and wrote scholarly works on geography and world history.

A CRACK IN THE ARMOR

After al-Mamun, the next two caliphs were al-Mutasim (reign 833–842) and al-Wathiq (reign 842–847). They promoted a policy that was to have unfortunate consequences for the Caliphate: they began expanding their armies with large numbers of Turkish slave soldiers called Mamluks. These soldiers formed the core of the caliph's palace guard in Baghdad. Eventually, they became powerful enough to make or break a caliph—in much the same way as the Praetorian Guard of the Roman Empire had possessed the power to support or effectively overthrow emperors. When the next caliph, al-Mutawakkil (reign 847–861), tried to reverse this policy, he was murdered by the Turkish guard and replaced by his son, al-Muntasir, who had conspired with the soldiers. Although the Turks con-

An illustrated page from a Mamluk manuscript, *Manual of Horsemanship*, copied in 1474 for an officer in charge of troop training. Mamluks, usually of Turkish descent, were originally slave soldiers who formed mercenary armies during the Middle Ages. They were particularly powerful in Egypt and Syria during the Mamluk Sultanate (1250–1517).

verted to Islam, the base of unity in Islam was gone: the army learned how to control the Caliphate, and the caliphs were soon reduced to little more than figureheads.

This weakening of the Caliphate led to a period when much of the empire was ruled by local dynasties. Early in the tenth century, the Buyids, soldiers of fortune from northwest Persia, set up a confederation to govern western Persia and Iraq. They established themselves in Baghdad in 945, and the Abbasid caliphs held office only because the Buyids allowed it.

CHAPTER 4

THE FATIMIDS AND THE DECLINE OF THE CALIPHATE

A group of Yemeni Shiites founded the Fatimid dynasty in the late tenth century. The Fatimids practiced Ismailism, a form of Shiism. They opposed the Sunni Caliphate of the Abbasid dynasty.

THE FATIMIDS IN CAIRO

From Yemen, the Fatimids expanded into North Africa and Sicily. In 909, al-Mahdi Billah (reign 909–934), proclaimed the dynasty a rival caliphate. The first four Fatimid caliphs ruled from Tunisia. After the Fatimids conquered Egypt in 969, they built a new capital, Cairo.

The dynasty eventually also controlled western Arabia (including Mecca and Medina), Syria, Palestine, and the Red Sea coast of Africa. In 1057–1059 the Fatimid caliph was briefly proclaimed in Baghdad. However, the Fatimids experienced much internal and external conflict.

The City of the Dead quarter of Cairo, Egypt.

Disputes over succession to the title of caliph led to the dynasty's collapse. The last Fatimid caliph died in 1171. The dynasty was succeeded by the Sunnite Ayyubid dynasty under the legendary Saladin, who supported the Abbasids.

EASTERN CRISES

The northeastern fringe of the Islamic world was governed until 999 by Samanid rulers, military commanders who gave only token allegiance to the caliphs.

THE LEGENDARY SALADIN

Born in 1137 or 1138 in Takrit, Mesopotamia (now in Iraq), Saladin grew up in Syria. As a teenager, he showed more inclination to become a Muslim scholar than a soldier. But when he finished school, he joined the staff of his uncle, an important military commander.

After his uncle's death in 1169, Saladin became commander of the Syrian troops in Egypt as well as vizier of the Fatimid caliph there. Two years later, Saladin abolished the Fatimid Caliphate of Egypt and became the country's sole ruler. He also changed the official branch of Islam in Egypt from Shiite to Sunni. Saladin then worked to unite Egypt, Syria, northern Mesopotamia, and Palestine under his

Saladin, first sultan of Egypt and Syria and the founder of the Ayyubid dynasty, is depicted here in a copy of a miniature painting, c. 1180.

rule. Using diplomacy by preference and military force only when necessary, he achieved that goal by 1186.

Saladin gained a reputation as a good but firm ruler. He devoted himself to the growth of Islam. He founded colleges and mosques. He supported Muslim scholars and preachers. He also encouraged all Muslims to unite against the Christian Crusaders.

In 1187, Saladin trapped and destroyed an army of Crusaders near Tiberias in northern Palestine. This victory allowed his armies to conquer most of the Crusader kingdom of Jerusalem, including Acre, Beirut, Nazareth, Jaffa, and Ascalon. In October, the city of Jerusalem surrendered to Saladin's army. His conquest was civilized and magnanimous.

Saladin's achievement spurred Europe to launch the Third Crusade, which failed to undo Saladin's conquests. After defeating the last of the new crusaders in October 1192, Saladin returned to Damascus. He died there in 1193.

The Samanids were replaced in the eleventh century by a Turkish military ruling class.

In the eastern section of the Caliphate, the powerful Ghaznavid empire was established by Turkish slave guards of the Samanids. Sultan Mahmud of Ghazna (reign 998–1030) assembled a powerful military force and incorporated territories extending from northern Persia and Central Asia to the Ganges basin in India. The Ghaznavids sought to legitimate themselves through strong ties to the caliphs.

From the eleventh century on, the whole Islamic empire was in a state of crisis. From the east came a new group of Turks, the Seljuqs, who converted to Islam but conquered most of the Muslim lands of the Middle East and parts of Anatolia (Asia Minor). Their success on the battlefield against the Byzantine Empire contributed to the decision by Christian Crusaders from western Europe to capture the Holy Land from the Muslims.

THE LAST ABBASIDS

The Crusaders were ultimately defeated. The Turkish empire disintegrated in the twelfth century, however, owing to succession disputes and rivalries between ambitious generals. For a time, the authority of the caliphs was reasserted, and the Abbasid caliph al-Nasir (reigned 1180–1225) became a central figure in the complex politics of the age. But by encouraging the invasion of the Mongols to overthrow the Turks, he unintentionally

This miniature painting of Mongol warriors was created for an Islamic history book, Rashid al-Din's *History of the World*, in 1307.

brought an end to the Abbasid Caliphate. The last Abbasid, al-Mustasim (reign 1242–1258), was unable to ward off the Mongol onslaughts led by Hulegu. In 1258 the Mongols raided Baghdad and killed the caliph and his family, effectively ending the Abbasid Caliphate.

A few years after the massacre, a man claiming to be of the Abbasid line appeared in Cairo. He was accepted as caliph by the Mamluk sultans, who had succeeded the Ayyubids, but he held no real power. This individual and his successors were removed from politics and from society in general by the Mamluks, who maintained actual power.

This state of affairs continued until 1517 when the Ottoman Empire defeated the Mamluks and moved the so-called caliphate to their capital in Constantinople (now Istanbul, Turkey). The office soon lapsed.

INVOKING THE CALIPHATE

The Ottoman sultans revived the idea of the caliphate in the eighteenth century, when their empire had lost territory and was declining. The Ottoman claim to leadership of the Islamic community served as a way for them to retain some influence over Muslim populations in lands that had earlier belonged to their empire. Their claim to the caliphate was also a means of strengthening Ottoman legitimacy within the empire. After the Ottoman Empire came to an end,

This photo shows the last caliph of Islam, Abdulmejid II, in exile in Bern, Switzerland, in 1924. He was dethroned following the foundation of the Turkish Republic by Mustafa Kemal Ataturk.

the Turkish republic formally dissolved the caliphate in 1924.

In subsequent years, Islamists occasionally invoked the caliphate as a symbol of global Islamic unity. In the twentieth and early twenty-first centuries, reestablishing the caliphate had not been of practical interest to mainstream Islamist groups such as the Muslim Brotherhood in Egypt. The caliphate did, however, figure prominently in the goals of the violent extremist group al-Qaeda.

In June 2014, an insurgent group known as the Islamic State in Iraq and the Levant (ISIL; also

Iraqi soldiers display a captured flag of the Islamic State on the outskirts of Mosul, Iraq, after retaking much of the eastern part of the city from jihadists in November 2016.

known as the Islamic State in Iraq and Syria [ISIS]), which had taken control of areas of eastern Syria and western Iraq, declared the establishment of a caliphate with the group's leader Abu Bakr al-Baghdadi as caliph. In accordance with that declaration, the group began referring to itself simply as "the Islamic State." The group's claims to universal leadership of the Muslim community were widely rejected by other Muslim groups.

ascetic Practicing strict self-denial as a measure of personal and especially spiritual discipline; strict in appearance, manner, or attitude.

assassinate To murder (usually a prominent person) by sudden or secret attack often for political reasons.

caliph A successor of Muhammad as temporal and spiritual head of Islam.

caliphate The office of a caliph or the land he rules over.

clan A group of people tracing descent from a common ancestor.

extremist One who advocates extreme measures or views and expresses support for ideas that are very far from what most people consider correct or reasonable.

fief A large area of land that was ruled over by a lord in medieval times; a feudal estate.

inherent Belonging to or being a part of the basic nature of a person or thing.

insurgent A person who revolts against civil authority or an established government.

Islamist A member of a reform movement advocating the reordering of government and society in accordance with laws prescribed by Islam.

magnanimous Showing or suggesting nobility of feeling and generosity of mind.

Muslim A person whose religion is Islam; a follower of Islam.

piety The quality or state of being pious, such as dutifulness in religion.

polemicist One who aggressively attacks or refutes the opinions or principles of another.

provincial To do with an administrative district or division of a country; the part or parts of a country far from the capital or chief city.

prudent Wise and careful in action or judgment.

secede To withdraw from an organization.

sect A group adhering to a distinctive doctrine or to a leader; a party or faction.

sultan A king or sovereign, especially of a Muslim state.

temporal Of or relating to earthly life; lay or secular rather than clerical or sacred.

vizier A high executive officer of various Muslim countries and especially of the Ottoman Empire.

Ahmad, Abdul Basit. *'Ali bin Abi Tâlib: The Fourth Caliph of Islam* (Golden Series of the Prophet's Companions). Riyadh, Saudi Arabia: Darussalam, 2004.

Ahmad, Abdul Basit, Aqeel Walkar, and Muhammad Ayub Sapra. *'Uthman bin Affan: The Third Caliph of Islam* (Golden Series of the Prophet's Companions). Riyadh, Saudi Arabia: Darussalam, 2004.

Campo, Juan Eduardo. *Encyclopedia of Islam* (Encyclopedia of World Religions). New York, NY: Facts on File, 2009.

Flatt, Lizann. *Early Islamic Empires* (Life in the Early Islamic World). New York, NY: Crabtree Publishing, 2013.

January, Brendan. *Arab Conquests of the Middle East* (Pivotal Moments in History). Minneapolis, MN: Twenty-First Century Books, 2009.

January, Brendan. *ISIS: The Global Face of Terrorism.* Minneapolis, MN: Twenty-First Century Books, 2017.

Kennon, Caroline, Seth Hughes, and Siyavush Saidian. *Rise of ISIS: The Modern Age of Terrorism.* New York, NY: Lucent Press, 2017.

Man, John. *Saladin: The Life, the Legend, and the Islamic Empire.* London, UK: Bantam Press, 2015.

Mujahid, Abdul Malik. *Golden Stories of 'Umar Ibn Al-Khattaab.* Riyadh, Saudi Arabia: Darussalam, 2012.

Nardo, Don. *The Birth of Islam* (World Religions and Beliefs). Greensboro, NC: Morgan Reynolds, 2012.

Nardo, Don. *The Islamic Empire*. Detroit, MI: Lucent Books, 2011.

Romanek, Trudee. *Government and Law in the Early Islamic World* (Life in the Early Islamic World). New York, NY: Crabtree Publishing, 2013.

Whiting, Jim. *The Role of Religion in the Early Islamic World* (Life in the Early Islamic World). New York, NY: Crabtree Publishing, 2012.

WEBSITES

Because of the changing nature of internet links, Rosen Publishing has developed an online list of websites related to the subject of this book. This site is updated regularly. Please use this link to access this list:

http://www.rosenlinks.com/EIMA/Islamic

INDEX